TABLE OF C...

1	ASSIGNMENT	
2	BIBLE	
3	CONVERSATION	5
4	DECISIONS	6
5	DIFFERENCE	7
6	DISOBEDIENCE	8
7	DREAMS	9
8	ENVIRONMENT	10
9	EXCELLENCE	11
10	FAITH	12
11	FAVOR	13
12	HARVEST	14
13	HOLY SPIRIT	15
14	HONOR	16
15	IDEAS	17
16	INSPIRATION	18
17	LEARNER	19
18	PRAYER	20
19	PROTOCOL	21
20	QUESTIONS	22
21	REACTIONS	23
22	RECEIVER	24
23	RELATIONSHIPS	25
24	SEED-SOWING	26
25	SERVANTHOOD	27
26	SUCCESS	28

Handwritten notes:
① Pray 7 min a day
② Pray in the H.S. Language. + Psm 23
+ Lords prayer
③

God can get me anywhere in the world in 24 hrs

Unless otherwise indicated, all Scripture quotations are taken from the King James Version of the Bible.

31 Days of Wisdom · ISBN 978-1-942709-23-7 · B-414

Copyright © 2015 by **MIKE MURDOCK**

All publishing rights belong exclusively to Wisdom International

Editor/Publisher: Deborah Murdock Johnson

Published by The Wisdom Center

4051 Denton Hwy. · Fort Worth, Texas 76117

1-817-759-BOOK · 1-817-759-2665 · 1-817-759-0300

MikeMurdockBooks.com

1 Your Assignment Is
Always The Problem
God Has *Designed* You
To Solve For Others.

2 An Uncommon Assignment
Attracts An
Uncommon Adversary.

3 *Divine* Provision Is
Only Guaranteed
At The *Place of
Your Assignment.*

4 You Will Never Be
Promoted
Until You Become
Over-Qualified For Your
Present Assignment.

5 What You *Hate*...
Is A Clue To What God
Has *Assigned* You To Do.

6 The Only Part of
The Bible That Is
Working For You Is
The Part You Have
Chosen To *Believe.*

7 Study Your *Bible...*
To Know *God.*
Study *Reactions...*
To Know *People.*
Study *Opportunities...*
To Know Your
Assignment.

8 The *Word* of God Is
The *Wisdom* of God.

9 Your *Reaction* To
The Word of God Is
A Picture of Your *Respect*
For God.

10 Those Who *Ask*
The Questions
Determine The *Quality* of
Every Conversation.

11 Your Seed Is
A *Conversation*
With God.

12 Every Miracle *Begins*
With A *Conversation*.

13 Disappointment Is
A *Conversation*
About Your Future.

14 Every Conversation Gives
Birth…To *Something;*
Perception, Change,
Doubt or Faith.

15 Every Decision *Reveals*
Your Faith...or
Your Doubt.

16 The Feeling You Desire
Is Usually
One Decision Away.

17 Failure Is Simply
The *Decision* To Quit.

18 Every Radical Change Is
One Decision Away.

19 Focus Is A Decision:
Your *Past* or
Your *Future*.

20 Never Make A
Permanent Decision
Because of A
Momentary Desire.

21 Your Significance Is Not
In Your *Similarity*
To Another, But In Your
Point of Difference
From Another.

22 Your Difference...Is
More *Important* Than
Your Weakness.

23 Your Difference...Is Whose
Happiness *Matters*
To You MOST.

24 The Difference In People
Is...What They Are
Unwilling To Live Without.

25 Never Study Your
Weakness...Study
Your *Difference*.

26 Disobedience Is Always
More Costly
Than Obedience.

27 The Waves of *Yesterday's*
Disobedience Will Splash
On The Shores of *Tomorrow*
For A Season.

28 God Will Never Advance
New Instructions
Beyond Your Last Act
of Disobedience.

29 The Divine *Explanation*
For Pain Is *Disobedience.*

30 Obedience Is The Only
Thing God Has Ever
Required of Man.

31 An Uncommon Dream
Requires Uncommon *Faith*.

32 Any God-Given Dream
Will *Require* God
To Achieve It.

33 Create Your Dream Wall
And Environment...
That Keeps You *Focused*
And *Motivated*.

34 Honor Is...The *Uninvested*
Price For Every
Unexperienced Dream.

35 When You Decide
What Will *Live*...
You Have Decided
What Will *Die*.

36 The Proof of Desire
Is *Pursuit*.

37 Every Environment Requires A Code of Conduct For *Entering* or *Remaining* In It.

38 Never Stay In An Environment That *Magnifies* Your Weakness.

39 When You Are Unable To Control Your *Environment...* Control Your *Focus.*

40 If You Don't *Control* Your Own Environment... Someone Else Will.

41 I Have Decided To Be... The *Environment.* Decide To HAPPEN... *Everywhere* You Are.

42 The Proof of Mediocrity
Is *The Resentment of Excellence.*

43 Deception...Gives Gifts To
Control Decisions.
Integrity...Gives Gifts To
Reward Excellence.

44 Excellence...
Is Always *Rewarded.*
Excellence...
Is *Addictive.*
Excellence...
Guarantees *Favor.*

45 Excellence...Makes Your
"Future" *Crave*
Your Presence.

46 Excellence...Does Not
Increase With *Age.*
Excellence Increases...
With *Integrity.*

47 The *Clearer* Your Goals,
The Greater Your *Faith*.

48 The Seasons of Your Life
Will Change *Every Time
You Use Your Faith*.

49 When *Fatigue* Walks In,
Faith Walks *Out*.

50 Your *Faith* Decides
Your *Miracles*.

51 Do You Really *Discern*
That Your "Faith" Is
Deciding The *Quality* of
Your Life?

52 Some Use Their Faith...
To *Endure* Their Life.
Some Use Their Faith...
To *Change* Their Life.

53 One Day of *Favor* Is Worth A Thousand Days of *Labor*.

54 Currents of Favor Begin To Flow The *Moment* You Solve A Problem For Someone.

55 Uncommon *Obedience* Unleashes Uncommon *Favor*.

56 *Instant* Obedience Is The Seed For *Instant* Favor.

57 The *Absence* of Favor Is The Proof You Do Not Belong.

58 Favor Is The *Currency* For Money.

59 Access Is Proof of *Favor*.

60 Every Seed Produces
A Harvest...
Good, Bad or *Nothing*.

61 Expectation Is The *Seed*
Every Harvest Obeys.

62 Forgiveness Must Become
Your *Seed* Before You
Reap It As A *Harvest*.

63 An Uncommon *Seed*
Always Creates
An Uncommon *Harvest*.

64 If What You Hold In Your
Hand Is Not Enough
To Be Your *Harvest,*
It Must Be Your *Seed*.

65 The Quality of Your *Seed*
Determines
The Quality of Your *Harvest*.

66 When You *Enter*
    The Secret Place,
You Become Involved With
    The Holy Spirit;
When You *Exit*
    The Secret Place,
He Becomes Involved
    With You.

67 The Holy Spirit Leaves
    Nobody...*Unwarned.*

68 The Holy Spirit...Is The
    Easiest Relationship
In My Life.
    The Only Person...
Who Requires No
    Explanations From Me.

69 The Holy Spirit...
    Is The Only *Person*
Capable of Being
    Contented With You.

70 Honor Is The *Seed*
For Longevity, of Life
or Relationships.

71 Honor Must Become
Your *Seed* Before
You Reap It As A *Harvest*.

72 Honor Is...
The *Willingness* To
Reward *Difference*.

73 The Only Person Who
Can Guarantee Your
Promotion Is *The One*
Whose Instructions
You Honor.

74 Wisdom *Discerns* The
Difference In Moments;
Honor Celebrates The
Difference In Moments;
Love Deposits Its Difference
In Moments.

75 Uncommon Pain...*Produces* Uncommon Ideas.

76 Happy People Are *Wonderful* For *Relationships.* Unhappy People Are Marvelous *Resources* For *Ideas.*

77 Happy Voices... Birth *Energy.* Unhappy Voices... Birth *Ideas.*

78 A Divine *Idea*...Is Not A Divine *Instruction.*

79 IDEAS...
1~*Create* A Tomorrow Room. (Pictures of Future Goals.)
2~*Choose* One Topic To Master.
3~*Keep* A List of Questions.

80 Romance...Whatever
Inspires You.
Cuddle It...In The Corners
of Your Mind.
Caress It...Smilingly.
It Is A *Fireplace.*

81 Life's Greatest *Skill:*
Keeping Yourself *Inspired.*

Life's Greatest *Habit:*
Recording Your
Thoughts Relentlessly.

82 Find The *Stream* of
Inspiration...And
Live There.

83 When You Are *Inspired...*
There Is *Nothing*
You Cannot Do.

84 And...The...*Winner*...Is...
Whoever Can *Keep*
Themselves *Inspired.*

85 The Learner...*Wakes Up*
A *Different* Person...
Every Single Day.

86 The *Mind*...of A *Learner.*
The *Heart*...of A *Warrior.*
The *Hands*...of A *Servant.*

87 Learners *Improve* Every
Single Day.

88 God Is Very *Attracted*
To...LEARNERS.

89 A Passionate Protégé
Gets *Unending Access.*

90 Learning Is Not...
A Place of Arrival...
But A Place of *Beginning*...
...of Changes.
...Decision-Making.

91 The Master Key To
Prayer Life...Is
*Unceasing Mutterings To
The Holy Spirit.*
Unending Conversation...
About Tasks...People.

92 God Does Not Respond To
Needs...Desires...
Pain...Concerns.
God *Responds* Only To
Your SPOKEN...
Prayer of Faith.

93 Prayer...Produces *Nothing.*
Prayer With Faith...
Produces *Everything.*

94 Worry...Is Not Prayer.
Anger...Is Not Prayer.
Pain...Is Not Prayer.
*Prayer...Is Conversation
With God.*

95 Protocol...You Have No
Idea How *Far* God
Would Take You...
If You Knew How To
Act When You Got There.

96 Protocol Is The
Expected Behavior
That *Communicates* Honor
And Importance
In An Environment.

97 *Protocol* Will Take You
Further Than *Genius.*

98 *Protocol* Is...
A Seed of *Honor.*

99 Ignored Protocol...
Destroys A Lifetime
of Favor.

100 Zeal Without *Protocol* Is...
Chaos.

101 The Most *Powerful* Thing On Earth Is...
          A Question.

102 Until You *Ask* A Question...
          Others *Control*
               Your Information.

103 Enough Questions...Make Your Decision-Making Easy.

104 The *Seed* For Instant
               Change Is...
          ...One More *Question*.

105 The *Unasked* Question...
          Keeps You *Poor*.

106 Changes In Your Life...
          ...Will Happen At The *Speed*
               of Your Questions.

107 Your Reaction...*Explains* Your Understanding.

108 FAVOR...Is Not A *Miracle.* FAVOR...Is A *Reaction.*

109 Reactions...*Control* Your *Success.*
Reactions To Opportunity...
To A Gift...
To An Instruction...
To Correction.

110 YOUR REACTIONS...
...*Explain* The Quality of Your *Caring.*

111 Your Reaction To My Problem...Is A Picture of Your Heart.

112 You Must *Become* A
World-Class *Receiver*...
BEFORE...
You Can *Become*...
A World-Class *Sower*.

Receive...Opportunities...Differences
...Ideas...Instructions...Correction.

113 Every Conversation
Contains A *Giver*...
And A *Receiver*.

114 What You Call A *Miracle*...
God Calls A *Gift*.
He Searches For...*Receivers*.

Are You Mastering The Art
of Receiving?

115 ECSTACY...To A Giver Is
Discovering Someone
Qualified To Receive.

116 It Is Your *Responsibility* To
Identify The Divine
Role of Every Relationship.

117 Odor In A Refrigerator...
Is *Explained* By
The Expiration Date.
Odor In A Relationship...
May Be *Explained*
The *Same Way*.

118 The Most Important
Person In Your Life...
Is The Person Who
Builds Your *Faith*.

119 Access...Is Not Relationship.
Access...Is *Opportunity* To
Qualify For Relationship.

120 Every Relationship...
Has *Rules*.
...Known or Unknown.
...Spoken or Unspoken.
...Ignored or Embraced.
...Honored or Dishonored.

121 My Challenges~
Sowing Seed...
Has Been *Easy* For Me.
Discerning Fertile Soil...
Has Been My
Greatest *Challenge.*

122 Seed-Faith Is *Sowing*
Something You Have
Been *Given* For
Something Else You
Have Been *Promised.*

123 God Gives Seed...
To *Sowers.*
God Gives Harvest...
To *Receivers.*

124 I *Believe*...In The Law
of The Seed.
It *Works* In My Life.

Whatever You Choose To
Believe...Is Working
For You, Too.

125 The Quality of Your
Servanthood Decides
The *Timing* of
Your Promotion.

126 You Can Only Be
Promoted By
The Person You Serve.

127 Your *Excellence* In
Servanthood Will
Decide *Where* You Are
Invited To Serve.

128 Servanthood Is
The Seed
For *Recognition.*

129 Servanthood Is
The Seed
For *Impartation.*

130 Servanthood *Decides*
The *Fragrance of The Palace.*

131 Success Is The *Fragrance of Joy* When A Goal Has Been Achieved.

132 The Key To Success Is *Not* Seeing How *Much* You Can Do, But Doing The *One Thing* You Love *Most*…With *Excellence.*

133 Success…Is A *Daily* Experience. You Alone…Can *Schedule* It.

134 Secrets-of-Life…*Decide* What Real "Success" Is…To YOU.

135 Your *Success* Is Determined By… Who *Likes* You. Your *Stress* Is Determined By… Who *Doesn't.*

136 Your Respect For *Time* Is A Prediction of Your *Financial* Future.

137 Never Give More Time To A *Critic* Than You Would Give To A *Friend*.

138 *Time* Will Expose What *Interrogation* Cannot.

139 Those Who Waste Your Time...Are *Enemies* To Your *Prosperity*.

140 Mentorship *Creates* Success Without The *Waiting* Time.

141 I Have Never Met A Poor Man... Who *Valued His Time*.

142 **C**_hoose_...
>3 Small Goals Today.
Magnify...
>In Your Mind.
Plan A Reward Time...
>Tonight.
Tell The Person...
>Who Rejoices With You.

143 **S**omething _Big_ Today May
>Be _Small_ Tomorrow.

144 **A**nother Day.
>Another..._Masterpiece_
In The Museum of My Life.
>_Every_ 24 Hours.
Another Masterpiece.
>I _Paint._

145 **E**very _Feeling_ You Are
>_Pursuing_ In Your Future
...Was _Hidden_ In Today.
>Did You Find It..?

146 Morning *Habit*...Alone
With The Word of God...
That's The Voice of God.

147 I Am *Addicted* To...
The Presence of God.
I Have A *Passion*...To *Learn*
From The Holy Spirit.
I Am A Misfit...Elsewhere.

148 The Price of God's Presence
Is *Time...In It.*

149 Those Who *Despise* The
Presence of God...
Are *Disqualified* For The
"Presents" of God.

150 Beautiful, Peaceful Day...
In The Presence of God.
"His Mind Is Kept In
Perfect Peace."
Focus...*Chooses* Our Feelings.

151 Move *Swiftly* When God Speaks To You And Instructs You To *Give*.

152 Your Decisions Decide Your *Wealth*.

153 Wealth Is When You Have A Lot of Something You *Love*.

154 Pursue The *Wisdom* And *Counsel* of Financial Advisors And Uncommon Financial Achievers.

155 Inspiration...Is The *Seed* For Wealth.

156 Embrace The Word of God As Your *Personal Financial Encyclopedia*.

157 **W**ISDOM...
~Is The Ability To *Discern*
DIFFERENCE...(In People,
Moments, Environments).
~Is The Ability To *Anticipate*
A Consequence or Reward.

158 **W**ISDOM Begins...One
Question From Now.

159 **W**isdom...Is *Brief.*
Opinions...Are *"Long."*

160 **W**isdom...Is *Knowing* The
Divine Reaction To A
Human Problem.

161 **E**very Problem...Is Simply
A Wisdom Problem.

162 **T**he *Secret Place*...Is The
Wisdom Place of Your Life.

*W*isdom Is...
Recognition of Difference.
Honor Is...
Rewarding of Difference.
Understanding Is...
Knowing The Value of
Difference.

-Mike Murdock

7 Decisions That Decide
Your Prosperity

Dr. Mike Murdock

*If you are willing + obedient
God will be in control of everything*

1 *Y*our Decision To Write Out A List of Specific Goals And Keep Them In Front of You Every Day.

2 *Y*our Decision To Become A Lifetime Learner. *Be excited, have passion*

3 *Y*our Decision To Show Honor To The Scriptural Chain of Authority. *Parents itll go well with you* *Promotion comes from someone whos above you*

4 *Y*our Decision To Excel In Solving Problems For Someone Who Is Trusting You.

5 *Y*our Decision To Make The Holy Spirit Your Lifetime Counselor.

6 *Y*our Decision To Pursue Mentorship From Uncommon Financial Achievers.

7 *Y*our Decision To Sow Seed Into The Work of God...With Persistent Expectation.

THE WISDOM CENTER
4051 Denton Highway · Fort Worth, TX 76117

1-817-759-BOOK
1-817-759-2665
1-817-759-0300

You Will Love Our Website..!
MikeMurdockBooks.com

35

My 7 Greatest Discoveries

1 *E*very Problem In Your Life Is Always A Wisdom Problem.

2 *T*he Most Important Thing You Can Do In Life Is Honor The Holy Spirit.

3 *G*od's Only Pain Is To Be Doubted, His Only Pleasure Is To Be Believed.

4 *W*hat You Make Happen For Others, God Will Make Happen For You.

5 *T*he Size of Your Enemy Decides The Size of The Rewards.

6 *Y*our Rewards Are Decided By The Problems You Choose To Solve For Others.

7 *A*n Uncommon Seed Always Creates An Uncommon Harvest.

THE WISDOM CENTER
4051 Denton Highway · Fort Worth, TX 76117
1-817-759-BOOK
1-817-759-2665
1-817-759-0300
— You Will Love Our Website..! —
MikeMurdockBooks.com

10 Facts About Your Assignment

1   **Everything God Created Was Created To Solve A Problem.**

2   **Your Assignment Is Always To A Person or To A People.**

  Your Assignment Is Not Your Decision, But Your *Discovery*.

3   **What You Hate Is A Clue To Something You Are Assigned To *Correct*.**

4   **What *Grieves* You Is A Clue To Something You Are Assigned To *Heal*.**

5   **What You Love Is A Clue To The Gifts, Skills And *Wisdom* You Contain.**

6   **Your Assignment Is *Geographical*.**

7   **Your Assignment Will Take You Where You Are *Celebrated* Instead of Tolerated.**

8   **Your Assignment Is Your Significant Difference From Others.**

9   **If You Rebel Against Your Assignment, God May Permit Painful Experiences To Correct You.**

10   **What You Love Most Is A Clue To Your Assignment.**

THE WISDOM CENTER
4051 Denton Highway · Fort Worth, TX 76117

1-817-759-BOOK
1-817-759-2665
1-817-759-0300

You Will Love Our Website..!
MikeMurdockBooks.com

37

21 FACTS ABOUT THE LAW OF THE SEED

1 There Will Never Be A Day In Your Life That You Have Nothing To Sow.

2 You Will Always Reap What You Sow.

3 Seed-Faith Is Sowing What You Have Been Given To Create What You Have Been Promised.

4 Your Seed Is Anything That Blesses Somebody.

5 The Law of The Seed (Sowing And Reaping) Was Intended To Birth Encouragement, Hope And Excitement Toward A Harvest.

6 Your Seed Is Any Tool God Has Given You To Create Your Future.

7 Something You Have Been Given By God Will Create Anything Else You Have Been Promised By God.

8 You Are A Walking Collection of Seeds.

9 Someone Near You Is "The Soil" Qualified To Receive Your Seed.

10 When You Let Go of What Is In Your Hand, God Will Let Go of What Is In His Hand.

11 Everything You Possess Is Something You Have Been Given.

12 If You Keep What You Presently Have, That Is The Most It Will Ever Be.

THE WISDOM CENTER
4051 Denton Highway · Fort Worth, TX 76117
1-817-759-BOOK
1-817-759-2665
1-817-759-0300
— You Will Love Our Website..! —
MikeMurdockBooks.com

13 When You Ask God For A Harvest, God Will Always Ask You For A Seed.

14 Your Seed Is The Only Proof You Have Mastered Greed.

15 When You Increase The Size of Your Seed, You Increase The Size of Your Harvest.

16 A Seed of Nothing Always Schedules A Season of Nothing.

17 Your Seed Must Always Be Comparable To The Harvest You Are Desiring.

18 Every Seed Contains An Invisible Instruction.

19 Your Seed Is Always Your Door Out of Trouble.

20 When You Give Your Seed An Assignment, You Are Giving Your Faith An Instruction.

21 Nothing Leaves Heaven Until Something Leaves Earth.

THE WISDOM CENTER 4051 Denton Highway · Fort Worth, TX 76117

1-817-759-BOOK
1-817-759-2665
1-817-759-0300

You Will Love Our Website..!
MikeMurdockBooks.com

39

7 Minutes With God

The Lord's Prayer

Matthew 6:9-13

Our Father Which Art In Heaven, Hallowed Be Thy Name. Thy Kingdom Come, Thy Will Be Done In Earth, As It Is In Heaven. Give Us This Day Our Daily Bread. And Forgive Us Our Debts, As We Forgive Our Debtors. And Lead Us Not Into Temptation, But Deliver Us From Evil: For Thine Is The Kingdom, And The Power, And The Glory, For Ever. Amen.

The Twenty-Third Psalm

The Lord Is My Shepherd; I Shall Not Want. He Maketh Me To Lie Down In Green Pastures: He Leadeth Me Beside The Still Waters. He Restoreth My Soul: He Leadeth Me In The Paths of Righteousness For His Name's Sake. Yea, Though I Walk Through The Valley of The Shadow of Death, I Will Fear No Evil: For Thou Art With Me; Thy Rod And Thy Staff They Comfort Me. Thou Preparest A Table Before Me In The Presence of Mine Enemies: Thou Anointest My Head With Oil; My Cup Runneth Over. Surely Goodness And Mercy Shall Follow Me All The Days of My Life: And I Will Dwell In The House of The Lord For Ever.

The
MIKE MURDOCK
Lifetime Library
eReader

A Treasury of Over 501 Books!

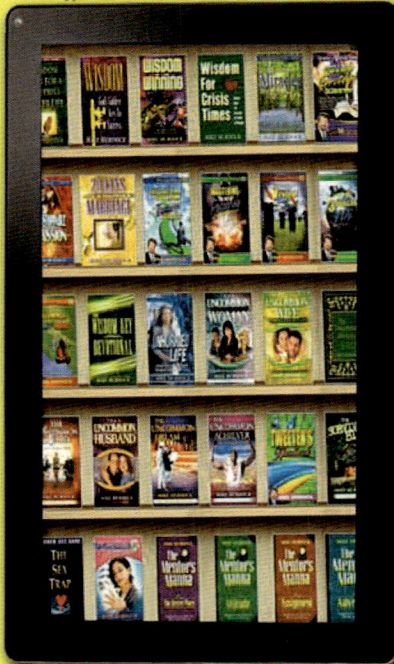

The MIKE MURDOCK Lifetime Library

1. 1-Minute Businessman's Devotional B-42
2. 1-Minute Businesswoman's Devotional B-43
3. 1-Minute Pocket Bible For Achievers B-50
4. 1-Minute Pocket Bible For Business Professionals B-62
5. 1-Minute Pocket Bible For Fathers B-51
6. 1-Minute Pocket Bible For Men B-60
7. 1-Minute Pocket Bible For Mothers B52
8. 1-Minute Pocket Bible For Teenagers B-53
9. 1-Minute Pocket Bible For Truckers B-63
10. 1-Minute Pocket Bible For Women B-61
11. 10 Decisions That Will Decide The Quality of Your Life BP-88
12. 10 Habits I Wish Every Protégé Knew, Part 2 BP-408
13. 10 Hours With Mike Murdock Day 1 BPN-1034
14. 10 Hours With Mike Murdock Day 2 BPN-1035
15. 10 Hours With Mike Murdock Day 3 BPN-1036
16. 10 Hours With Mike Murdock Day 4 BPN-1037
17. 10 Keys To A Successful Ministry BPN-1021
18. 10 Kinds of People You Will Need In The Garden of Your Success BP-145
19. 10 Master Keys In Excelling As An Effective Teacher B-291
20. 10 Most Important Words of A Millionaire BP-823
21. 10 Steps To Swift Prosperity, Part 1 BP-970-1
22. 10 Steps To Swift Prosperity, Part 2 BP-970-2
23. 10 Steps To Swift Prosperity, Part 3 BP-970-3
24. 10 Things Men Want In A Woman BP-1010
25. 10 Things That Matter In This Global Financial Crisis (Vol. 1) BP-311-1
26. 10 Things That Matter In This Global Financial Crisis (Vol. 2) BP-311-2
27. 10 Things That Matter In This Global Financial Crisis (Vol. 3) BP-311-3
28. 10 Things That Matter Most BP-362
29. 10 Things That Matter Most In A Financial Crisis, CUP
30. 10 Things That Matter Most In A Financial Crisis, Part 1 BPN-1026
31. 10 Things That Matter Most In A Financial Crisis, Part 2 BPN-1027
32. 10 Things That Matter Most In A Financial Crisis, Part 3 BPN-1028
33. 10 Things That Matter Most In A Financial Crisis, Part 4 BPN-1029
34. 10 Things That Matter Most In A Financial Crisis, Part 5 BPN-1030
35. 10 Things That Matter Most In A Financial Crisis, Part 6 BPN-1031
36. 10 Things You Must Do To Be A Millionaire for God, Part 1 BP-986-1
37. 10 Things You Must Do To Be A Millionaire for God, Part 3 BP-986-3
38. 10 Things You Must Do To Be A Millionaire for God, Part 5 BP-986-5
39. 10 Things You Must Do To Be A Millionaire for God, Part 6 BP-986-6
40. 10 Words That Will Be Important In The Next 24 Months BPN-1007
41. 101 Wisdom Keys B-45
42. 1,001 Wisdom Keys B-293

43. 12 Decisions That Will Decide The Quality of Your Life BP-239
44. 12 Ingredients of A Perfect Day, Vol. 1 BP-258-1
45. 12 Ingredients of A Perfect Day, Vol. 2 BP-258-2
46. 12 Proofs of Love BP-10
47. 12 Rewards of An Instruction BPN-1020
48. 16 Facts About The Presence of God B-61
49. 17 Facts About Thankfulness B-206
50. 121 Facts Every Tither Should Remember BP-336
51. 2 Minute Wisdom, Vol. 1 B-246
52. 2 Minute Wisdom, Vol. 2 B-247
53. 2 Minute Wisdom, Vol. 3 B-248
54. 2 Minute Wisdom, Vol. 4 B-249
55. 2 Minute Wisdom, Vol. 5 B-250
56. 20 Power Forces For A Successful Life, Part 1 BP-351
57. 20 Power Forces For A Successful Life, Part 4 BP-354
58. 21 Miracle Keys You Must Remember BP-370
59. 22 Life Keys My Father Taught Me BP-324
60. 22 Reactions That Reveal Character BP-283
61. 24 Facts You Should Know About Miracles BP-158
62. 25 Decisions That Will Birth The Uncommon Life BP-74
63. 25 Things That Will Improve Your Life, BP-147
64. 25 Things That Will Improve Your Life, BP-282
65. 25 Ways To Improve Your Life In 2005 BPN-1033
66. 25 Ways To Improve Yourself BP-35
67. 3 Forces of Life TT-102
68. 3 Must Haves For Preachers BP-991
69. 3 Ways To Simplify Your Life BP-357
70. 31 Facts About Wisdom B-46
71. 31 Greatest Chapters In The Bible B-54
72. 31 Keys To A New Beginning B-48
73. 31 Qualities of An Uncommon Mother BPN-1022
74. 31 Reasons I'm In Love With Jesus BP-47
75. 31 Reasons People Do Not Receive Their Financial Harvest B-82
76. 31 Scriptures Every Businesswoman Should Memorize B-193
77. 31 Scriptures Every Father Should Memorize B-180
78. 31 Scriptures Every Husband Should Memorize B-190
79. 31 Scriptures Every Leader Should Memorize B-189
80. 31 Scriptures Every Mother Should Memorize B-174
81. 31 Scriptures Every Teen Should Memorize B-185
82. 31 Secrets For Career Success B-44
83. 31 Success Words I Wish Every Protege Knew BP-958
84. 31 Things You Will Need To Become A Millionaire, Vol. 1 BP-116-1

85. 31 Things You Will Need To Become A Millionaire, Vol. 2 BP-116-2
86. 31 Wisdom Keys For Achieving The Uncommon Dream Within You BP-115
87. 365 Wisdom Keys of Mike Murdock B-229
88. 4 Overlooked Keys To Unleashing Prosperity BP-63
89. 44 Facts About Writing BPN-1038
90. 5 Keys To Birthing Your Daily Habit of Prayer BP-85
91. 5,001 Wisdom Quotations B-318
92. 69th Birthday Celebration BP-400
93. 7 Action Steps To Increase Your Daily Pleasure BP-229
94. 7 Areas Where You Should Excel In Wisdom BP-367
95. 7 Business Secrets of Jesus That Guarantee The Success of Your Business BP-218
96. 7 Crisis You Must Survive On Your Journey To Greatness, Part 2 BP-329
97. 7 Deadliest Mistakes You Can Make BP-193
98. 7 Deadly Mistakes You Can Change In A Day BP-1002
99. 7 Deadly Poisons That Can Destroy Greatest Team TT-82
100. 7 Decisions Necessary To Create A Successful Year BP-347
101. 7 Decisions That Control The Flow of Favor In Your Life, Vol. 1 BP-137-1
102. 7 Decisions That Control The Flow of Favor In Your Life, Vol. 2 BP-1137-2
103. 7 Decisions That Decide Your Wealth, Vol. 1 BP-109-1
104. 7 Decisions That Decide Your Wealth, Vol. 2 BP-109-2
105. 7 Decisions That Determine Your Personal Success BP-173
106. 7 Decisions That Will Decide Your Financial Wealth BP-109
107. 7 Decisions That Will Decide Your Success B-295
108. 7 Decisions That Will Decide Your Success BP-366
109. 7 Decisions That Will Get You Through The Dark Times BP-304
110. 7 Decisions That Will Make You Unstoppable In 2009 BP-297
111. 7 Divine Secrets Hidden In 9-11 BP-395
112. 7 Facts About The Seed BP-349
113. 7 Facts You Must Know About People To Succeed, Vol. 1A BP-206-1
114. 7 Facts You Must Know About People To Succeed, Vol. 1B BP-206-2
115. 7 Fascinating Qualities of The Jesus I Know BP-344
116. 7 Forces For Supernatural Success BP-48
117. 7 Hidden Ingredients In Every Miracle B-280
118. 7 Hidden Keys To Favor (SOW on Favor Vol. 17) B-119
119. 7 Immediate Rewards of Tithing B-264
120. 7 Important Facts You Should Know In Discerning Untrustworthy People BP-211
121. 7 Keys For Succeeding In The Workplace B-363

122. 7 Keys To 1,000 Times More B-104
123. 7 Keys To A Financial Breakthrough, Vol. 1 BP-28-1
124. 7 Keys To A Financial Breakthrough, Vol. 2 BP-28-2
125. 7 Keys To Achieving Your Ministry Dreams And Goals BPN-1001
126. 7 Keys To Becoming A Man of Excellence BP-227
127. 7 Keys To Keeping A Good Friendship TT-72
128. 7 Keys To Restoration After Your Life Losses BP-310
129. 7 Keys To Your Healing (SOW on Healing) B-120
130. 7 Kinds of People Who Always Fail TT-159
131. 7 Kinds of Men God Is Looking For BP-225
132. 7 Laws I Wish Every Protégé Knew BP-356
133. 7 Laws of Success In Your Life BPN-1006
134. 7 Laws That Will Affect Your Favor, Part 1 BP-343-1
135. 7 Laws That Will Affect Your Favor, Part 2 BP-343-2
136. 7 Laws You Must Honor To Create Uncommon Success, Vol. 2 BP-327
137. 7 Laws You Must Honor To Have Uncommon Success B-294
138. 7 Laws You Must Master To Receive The Blessings of God BP-272
139. 7 Master Keys In Becoming A Man of Worship BP-233
140. 7 Master Keys To Developing Your Self-Confidence BP-180
141. 7 Master Keys To Living In Financial Peace BP-117
142. 7 Master Keys To Uncommon Excellence BP-217
143. 7 Men Who Learned The Secret of Pleasuring God And The Rewards They Received BP-210
144. 7 Mistakes That Destroy The Bridge of Access BP-163
145. 7 Most Important People In Your Financial Life BP-199
146. 7 Necessary Conversations That Must Occur On Your Journey To Greatness, Part 3 BP-332
147. 7 Opportunities That You Must Never Overlook In Your Journey To Greatness, Part 5 BP-334
148. 7 Overlooked Keys To Effective Goal-Setting (SOW on Goal-Setting) B-127
149. 7 People Skills You Should Learn From The Life of Jesus BP-346
150. 7 Persuasions That Have Sustained Me BP-301
151. 7 Questions Every Man Should Ask Himself BP-223
152. 7 Questions That Reveal Your True Financial Passion BP-205
153. 7 Questions You Should Ask Yourself During A Crisis BP-174
154. 7 Reasons I Fell In Love With Jesus BP-138
155. 7 Revelations That Dramatically Changed My Life BP-246
156. 7 Rewards of Problem-Solving (SOW on Problem-Solving, Vol. 16) B-118
157. 7 Rewards of The Secret Place BP-84
158. 7 Rituals of Honor That Guarantee The Favor of God B-285
159. 7 Secrets From 7 Men Who Knew How To Obtain Miracles From God BP-232

160. 7 Secrets I Learned Personally From Dr. Oral Roberts BP-213
161. 7 Secrets My Mother Taught Me! BP-08
162. 7 Secrets of Men Who Endured BP-234
163. 7 Signposts To Your Assignment (SOW on Your Assignment) B-122
164. 7 Small Changes That Create Big Rewards in Your Financial Life BP-203
165. 7 Small Secrets That Will Unleash Your Supernatural Year BP-127
166. 7 Steps To Changing Your Life B-221
167. 7 Steps To Writing A Book BPN-1004
168. 7 Success Systems For Your Life BP-400
169. 7 Things A Man Can Do To Build A Strife Free Home BP-194
170. 7 Things Every Child Should Expect From Their Father BP-361
171. 7 Things Every Man Must Recognize To Create Uncommon Success BP-226
172. 7 Things Every Man Needs To Know About Celebrating BP-215
173. 7 Things Every Man Should Know About Himself BP-299
174. 7 Things Every Man Should Remember About Pain BP-212
175. 7 Things Every Successful Man Must Know About His Money BP-189
176. 7 Things I Wish Every Man Knew BP-302
177. 7 Things I Would Do Differently If I Could Begin My Ministry Over Again BPN-1005
178. 7 Things Jesus Conquered BP-995
179. 7 Things No Man Must Ever Forget BP-202
180. 7 Things That Matter To A Woman BP-186
181. 7 Things That Matter To God BP-278
182. 7 Things That Should Matter To A Man BP-231
183. 7 Things That Will Guarantee You A Raise BP-1038
184. 7 Things To Do When You Become Discouraged With The Christian Life BP-207
185. 7 Things To Look For In Your Friendships With Other Men BP-219
186. 7 Things To Remember On Your Journey To Greatness, Part 1 BP-328
187. 7 Things You Must Protect On Your Journey to Greatness BP-337
188. 7 Things You Should Do During This Financial Crisis BP-303
189. 7 Traps You Must Avoid On Your Journey To Greatness BP-336
190. 7 Uncomfortable Things A Man Must Do To Live An Uncommon Life BP-201
191. 7 Unstoppable Blessings You Should Expect In 2007 BP-208
192. 7 Ways Every Man Must Teach His Family BP-209
193. 7 Ways I Confront And Conquer The Spirit of Hopelessness BP-204
194. 7 Ways My Mother Changed My Life BP-316
195. 7 Ways To Increase Your Love Environment TT-61
196. 7 Ways to Simplify In 2010 BP-348
197. 7 Ways You Can Honor Your Mother BP-358
198. 7 Ways You Can Simplify Your Journey To Greatness BP-335

199. 7 Ways You Could Be A Blessing To Your Church BP-214
200. 7 Wealth-Whispers That Changed My Life BP-1011
201. 777 Tweets Uncensored B-341
202. A.S.K. - The Key To Life BP-907
203. Adaptation: The Golden Key To The World of Favor BP-101
204. Are You Asking The Right Questions..? BP-978
205. Attentiveness BP-1037
206. Battle Techniques For War-Weary Saints B-07
207. Becoming The Law of Process TT-15
208. Becoming The Man That Nobody Can Stop BP-162
209. Born To Taste The Grapes B-65
210. Building Credibility With A Leader BP-1006
211. Burden or Burden-Bearer TT-59
212. Character TT-84
213. Create Your Information Center BP-1046
214. Creating Tomorrow Through Seed-Faith B-06
215. Customize Your Life, Part 1 BP-1054-1
216. Customize Your Life, Part 2 BP-1054-2
217. Decisions... BP-908
218. Don't Permit Disrespect In Your Environment, Part 1 BP-1102-1
219. Don't Permit Disrespect In Your Environment, Part 2 BP-1102-2
220. Don't Stay Where You Are Not Received BP-1030
221. Dr. Mike Murdock & Ms. Viviana - How To Handle The Legal Zone of Your Life BP-1025
222. Dr. Mike Murdock & Ms. Viviana - The Preacher And The Law BP-1023
223. Dr. Mike Murdock & Ms. Viviana - Women In A Jam BP-1024
224. Dream Seeds B-11
225. Enduring Perplexing Seasons On Your Journey To Greatness - Part 4 BP-333
226. Enjoying The Winning Life B-08
227. Establish Your Harvest BP-832
228. Fathers and Sons and Daughters BPN-1003
229. Finding Your Purpose In Life B-05
230. Five Steps Out of Depression B-02
231. For Women Only..! The Spirit, The Man, The Money, Part 1 BP-992-1
232. For Women Only..! The Spirit, The Man, The Money, Part 2 BP-992-2
233. Forever Yours B-331
234. Four Forces That Guarantee Career Success B-09
235. Get Involved In Your Inspiration BP-1021
236. Getting Things Done Through People Who Don't Care B-000U
237. God's Golden Key To Success B-71
238. Greed, Gold And Giving B-66

239. Habits of Prosperity BP-1048
240. Honor: The Seed That Secures The Palace / The Secret Power of Honor In Your Private World, Part 1 BP-168-1
241. Honor: The Seed That Secures The Palace / The Secret Power of Honor In Your Private World, Part 2 BP-168-2
242. Honor: The Seed That Secures The Palace / The Secret Power of Honor In Your Private World, Part 3 BP-168-3
243. How Do You Qualify For A Miracle BP-444
244. How I Turned The Worst Day of My Life Into The Best Day of My Life BP-134
245. How To Be Trained For The Palace BP-949
246. How To Build An Effective Team BP-999
247. How To Build Your Womanly Self-Confidence BP-1001
248. How To Double Your Financial Support For Your Ministry BP-1012
249. How To Double Your Productivity In 24 Hours (SOW on Productivity) B-137
250. How To Excel In The Workplace BP-818
251. How To Have The Greatest Year In Your Lifetime, Collection BP-223
252. How To Hire People To Work For You BP-1036
253. How To Initiate A Date With A Man BP-1124
254. How To Make Yourself A Jesus Experience In Someone's Life BP-221
255. How To Master The Art of Receiving BP-359A
256. How To Read Your Bible BP-222
257. How To Receive The Word of God BP-975
258. How To Save Time BP-959
259. How To Survive A Personal Offense BP-964
260. How To Survive The Struggle With The Fools In Your Life BP-216
261. How To Talk To A Man BP-475
262. How To Turn Your Mistakes Into Miracles B-56
263. How To Get Your Boss To Like You BP-988
264. If I Had 27 Minutes Left To Live Collection BP-967
265. If You Were My Daughter B-364
266. Is Your Mouth Closing Doors of Favor..? BP-966
267. Is Your Mouth Making You Money? Collection B-000U
268. Just Give It To Jesus BP-185
269. Kingdom Investors BP-1051
270. Know The Uniqueness of Your Gift BP-1044
271. Know Those Who Labor Among You BP-985
272. Know Who To Invest In BP-1005
273. Know Who Walks Beside You B-000U
274. Know Your Investments BP-902
275. Love Matters B-389
276. Mastering The Art of Receiving TT-183
277. Mastering The Art of Receiving, Part 1 BP-359A
278. Mastering The Art of Receiving, Part 2 BP-359B

279. Mistakes Women Make BP-1020
280. Money Thoughts BP-963
281. Mother Talk BP-996
282. Mothers...Reach A Little Higher! B-343
283. My 7 Greatest Discoveries BP-298
284. My Biggest Mistakes In Ministry BP-1019
285. My Journey To Prosperity B-406
286. Offering Lesson From TWC Pulpit BPN-1024
287. One-Liners For Preachers BP-1018
288. Pastoral Talk BPN-1023
289. Power Bytes For The Productive Life B-000U
290. Protégé-Talk eB-308
291. Proximity Determines Who Sees You...Determines Everything BP-1123
292. Questions Every Man Should Ask Himself Making Major Decisions In Life BP-321
293. Reactions, Part 1 BP-1026-1
294. Reactions, Part 2 BP-1026-2
295. Rename, Focus And Restore BP-849
296. School of The Holy Spirit, Part 1 BPN-1008
297. School of The Holy Spirit, Part 2 BPN-1009
298. School of The Holy Spirit, Part 3 BPN-1010
299. School of The Holy Spirit, Part 4 BPN-1012
300. School of The Holy Spirit, Part 5 BPN-1013
301. Secrets of The Journey, Volume 1 B-92
302. Secrets of The Journey, Volume 2 B-93
303. Secrets of The Journey, Volume 3 B-94
304. Secrets of The Journey, Volume 4 B-95
305. Secrets of The Journey, Volume 5 B-96
306. Secrets of The Journey, Volume 6 B-102
307. Secrets of The Journey, Volume 7 B-103
308. Secrets of the Richest Man Who Ever Lived B-99
309. Seeds of Wisdom Collection...For The Spirit-Filled Life B-000U
310. Seeds of Wisdom On Adversity B-21
311. Seeds of Wisdom On Dream & Goals B-13
312. Seeds of Wisdom On Enemies, Vol. 22 B-124
313. Seeds of Wisdom On Habits B-18
314. Seeds of Wisdom On Mentorship, Vol. 24 B-126
315. Seeds of Wisdom On Miracles B-15
316. Seeds of Wisdom On Obedience B-20
317. Seeds of Wisdom On Overcoming, Vol. 5 B-17
318. Seeds of Wisdom On Prayer B-23
319. Seeds of Wisdom On Prosperity, Vol. 10 B-22
320. Seeds of Wisdom On Relationships B-14

321. Seeds of Wisdom On Seed-Faith B-16
322. Seeds of Wisdom On The Power of Words, Vol. 26 B-128
323. Seeds of Wisdom On Time-Management B-121
324. Seeds of Wisdom On Warfare B-19
325. Serious About Money BP-000U
326. Servanthood BP-1029
327. Seven Obstacles To Abundant Success B-64
328. Sex, Money and Marriage, Part 1 BP-976-1
329. Sex, Money And Marriage, Part 2 BP-976-2
330. Shed Your Load BP-1058
331. Should I Let The Baby Drown? BP-122
332. Sister-Talk BP-989
333. So...You Want To Be My Personal Assistant? BP-1003
334. Seeds of Wisdom - Seeds of Honor BP-1016
335. Studying The Bible BP-982
336. Success Tips That Will Cause You To Succeed With Your Life BP-906
337. Ten Lies Many People Believe About Money B-04
338. The 12 Step Formula For Restoring The Joy In Your Private World BP-258
339. The 3 Greatest Persuasions of Your Life BP-89
340. The 3 Greatest Turning-Points In My Life BP-38
341. The 3 Most Important Things In Your Life B-101
342. The 7 Deadly Mistakes A Man Can Make BP-1002
343. The 7 Foundations of The Blessed Life BP-364
344. The 7 Hidden Laws of Business BP-198
345. The 7 Life Philosophies That Have Changed My Life BP-368
346. The 7 Part-Formula For An Uncommon Life BP-325
347. The Assignment - Legacy Edition B-232
348. The Assignment Part 4, 7 Questions You Should Be Asking About Your Assignment BP-394
349. The Assignment Part 5, 7 Ways To Overcome Stagnation In Your Assignment BP-396
350. The Assignment Vol. 1: The Dream & The Destiny B-74
351. The Assignment Vol. 2: The Anointing & The Adversity B-75
352. The Assignment Vol. 3: The Trials & The Triumphs B-97
353. The Assignment Vol. 4: The Pain & The Passion B-98
354. The Blessing Bible B-28
355. The Book That Changed My Life B-117
356. The Bridge Called Divorce B-10
357. The Businessman's Topical Bible B-33
358. The Businesswoman's Topical Bible B-156
359. The Covenant of Fifty-Eight Blessings B-47
360. The Craziest Instruction God Ever Gave Me B-151
361. The Double Diamond Daily Devotional B-72

362. The Double Diamond Principle B-39
363. The Eagle 10 Lifestyle B-339
364. The Father's Topical Bible B-35
365. The Four Stages of A Successful Life BP-80
366. The Gift of Wisdom For Achievers B-68
367. The Gift of Wisdom For Brides B-88
368. The Gift of Wisdom For Champions B-67
369. The Gift of Wisdom For Fathers B-77
370. The Gift of Wisdom For Graduates B-87
371. The Gift of Wisdom For Grooms B-89
372. The Gift of Wisdom For Husbands B-84
373. The Gift of Wisdom For Leaders B-86
374. The Gift of Wisdom For Ministers B-90
375. The Gift of Wisdom For Mothers B-70
376. The Gift of Wisdom For Teenagers B-85
377. The Gift of Wisdom For Wives B-83
378. The Gift of Wisdom, Vol. 1 B-41
379. The God Book B-26
380. The Grandparent's Topical Bible B-34
381. The Greatest Day of My Life (SOW on The Holy Spirit, Vol. 14) B-116
382. The Greatest Success Habit On Earth B-80
383. The Greatness of Women And Their Lack of Training To Train BP-1049
384. The High Cost of Lost Favor Collection BP-1016
385. The High Cost of Untrained Staff BP-1041
386. The Holy Spirit Handbook B-100
387. The Imagination BP-192
388. The Importance of Prosperity BP-743
389. The Importance of Valuing Time BP-823
390. The Inmate's Topical Bible B-176
391. The Instruction You Follow Determines The Future You Create BP-877-7
392. The Jesus Book B-27
393. The Job Descriptions of The First Two People You Need To Hire BP-1004
394. The Jonah Story: Know Where You Belong BP-961
395. The Law of Honor…In The Success Equation, Part 2 BP-313
396. The Law of Honor…The Highest Law of Life, Part 1 BP-312
397. The Law of Order BP-281
398. The Law of Pleasure BP-909
399. The Law of Recognition B-114
400. The Law of Recognition: What Opportunities Are You Missing..? BP-971
401. The Leadership Secrets of Jesus B-91
402. The Magical Secrets of Goal-Setting BP-372
403. The Making of A Champion B-59
404. The Management of Your Finances BP-998

405. The Master Secrets of Making World-Class Decisions BP-995
406. The Mentor's Manna On Abilities B-73
407. The Mentor's Manna On Achievement B-79
408. The Mentor's Manna On Adversity B-81
409. The Mentor's Manna On Assignment B-76
410. The Mentor's Manna On Attitude B-58
411. The Mentor's Manna On The Secret Place B-78
412. The Millionaire Woman BP-983
413. The Minister's Topical Bible B-32
414. The Miracle Seed of Honor BP-940
415. The Mistakes I Have Made Over The Years, Part 1 BP-1055-1
416. The Mother's Topical Bible B-36
417. The Mystery & The Miracle of The Prosperity Gospel BP-23
418. The New Believer's Topical Bible B-37
419. The Proverbs 31 Woman B-49
420. The Qualities of The Eagles I Need In My Life BP-355
421. The Quickest Exit Out of A Crisis BP-1007
422. The Seeds of Wisdom Topical Bible B-31
423. The Sex Trap B-03
424. The Survival Bible B-29
425. The Systems of Success BP-1000
426. The Teen's Topical Bible B-30
427. The Tither's Topical Bible B-218
428. The Traveler's Topical Bible B-139
429. The Turning-Points of My Life BP-1022
430. The Tweeter's Handbook, Vol. 1 B-297
431. The Uncommon Achiever B-133
432. The Uncommon Dream B-135
433. The Uncommon Father B-131
434. The Uncommon Husband B-211
435. The Uncommon Leader B-106
436. The Uncommon Minister, Vol. 1 B-107
437. The Uncommon Minister, Vol. 2 B-108
438. The Uncommon Minister, Vol. 3 B-109
439. The Uncommon Minister, Vol. 4 B-110
440. The Uncommon Minister, Vol. 5 B-111
441. The Uncommon Minister, Vol. 6 B-112
442. The Uncommon Minister, Vol. 7 B-113
443. The Uncommon Minister English B-241
444. The Uncommon Mother B-132
445. The Uncommon Wife B-210
446. The Uncommon Woman B-146
447. The Unhurried Life B-230

448. The Widow's Topical Bible B-38
449. The Will of God Is Everything BP-812
450. The Wisdom Commentary, Vol. 1 B-136
451. The Wisdom Key Devotional B-165
452. The Wisdom Library of Mike Murdock, Vol. 1 B-144
453. The Wisdom Library of Mike Murdock, Vol. 2 B-175
454. The Wisdom Library of Mike Murdock, Vol. 3 B-188
455. The Wisdom Library of Mike Murdock, Vol. 4 B-199
456. The Wisdom Library of Mike Murdock, Vol. 5 B-200
457. The Wisdom Library of Mike Murdock, Vol. 6 B-272
458. The Wisdom Library of Mike Murdock, Vol. 7 B-273
459. The Wisdom Library of Mike Murdock, Vol. 8 B-274
460. The Wisdom Notes of Mike Murdock 2 B-303
461. The Wisdom Notes of Mike Murdock 3 B-311
462. The Wisdom Notes of Mike Murdock 7 B-320
463. The Wisdom Quotations of Mike Murdock, Volume 1 B-302
464. Things I Wish Somebody Would Have Told Me BP-956
465. Things That Matter Most - Reactions BP-374
466. Things That Matter Most During This Global Financial Crisis BP-308
467. Things That Will Help You Be Stress Free BP-1045
468. Things That Will Improve Your Assignment BP-974
469. Things That Will Trigger A Season of Prosperity In Your Life BP-1126
470. Thirty-One Secrets of An Unforgettable Woman B-57
471. Thoughts On Listening BP-896
472. Time-Management BP-981
473. To Find The Likeability of God TT-161
474. Training People In Your Life BP-1042
475. Trustworthiness, Vol. 1 BP-282
476. Twenty Keys To A Happier Marriage B-55
477. Uncommon Wisdom For An Uncommon Life B-000U
478. Unstoppable Passion B-224
479. Vashti Doesn't Live Here Anymore B-394
480. Warrior-Talk B-307
481. Wealth-Whispers, 31 Day Devotional B-000U
482. What Are The Problems You Love To Solve? BP-1039
483. What I Want You To Know BP-979
484. What I Was Slow To Learn BP-1052
485. What I Wish Every Protégé Knew, Part 1 BP-338
486. What I Wish Every Protégé Knew, Part 2 BP-339
487. What I Wish Every Protégé Knew, Part 3 BP-341
488. What I Wish Every Protégé Knew About The Law of Pursuit BP-356
489. What I Wish Men Knew About Money BP-428
490. What To Do To Avoid Unthankfulness In Your Life BP-1035

WHY I LOVE JESUS

God's Book, the Bible says, "For God So Loved The World, That He Gave His Only Begotten Son That Whosoever Believeth In Him Should Not Perish, But Have Everlasting Life," (John 3:16). Jesus loves you very much and wants to help you be the best person you can be. But, it is your choice if you want Jesus to be the King of your life.

To make Jesus the King of your life all you have to do is talk to Jesus by praying the following prayer: *"Dear Jesus, I ask You to come into my life today, and to forgive me for anything I have done that was not good. I believe that You died for me and that You will forgive me when I do wrong things. Thank You for Your love and forgiveness. I love You, Jesus, and I accept You now as the King of my life and the Ruler of my heart. In Jesus' name. Amen."*

Remember to talk to Jesus every day. Tell Him that you love Him and anything else you want Him to know. Always remember how much Jesus loves you!

☐ Yes, Mike! I prayed to Jesus today and asked Him to be the King of my life. Please send me my free gift of your book *"31 Keys To A New Beginning"* to help me with my new life in Christ.

Name _____ Birthdate ___ / ___

Address _____

City _____ State _____ Zip _____

Phone (___) _____ E-Mail _____

Mail To: **The Wisdom Center**
4051 Denton Hwy. Fort Worth, TX 76117
1-817-759-0300
Website: MikeMurdockBooks.com

56